To Ryan's mama, Lauren

Donna Pattillo

Skunk Feathers

by

Donna Pattillo

and a bunch of kids who had the nerve to grow up while I was thinking about writing this book.

Skunk Feathers

A book of stories, questions,
pictures, conversations, definitions, opinions,
and tattles... straight from the second grade.

Dedicated to the children
who have passed through my classroom on the
way to other times and places.

You have filled my life with love, laughter, and
little snippets of wisdom
which can only come from those who see
and hear with their hearts.

Thank you,

Mrs. Pattillo

In memory of
Mr. Otis LaVerne Damron
who did not fire me

Skunk Feather: (n) A black and white feather found only on the Tunnel Hill Elementay School playground, and once by the lake at the "Chattanooga Natchur Sinner" where we went for a field trip. Some people believe they have magical powers.

Teaching is an adventure ...

When you are the teacher of small children, you need to have the ability to laugh at yourself, and to yourself, without letting a single giggle escape. Something is going to happen everyday. You can count on it. For instance, could YOU keep a straight face if your day started this way?

"Danny," I asked, "Why have you been absent for the last two days?"

To which Danny unabashedly replied,

"I had the shits."

I pretended to drop something under my desk, and didn't come up until I got myself under control.

And then there was the time ...

Jimmy came after school to work on the computer. He was trying to get to Reader's Workshop so that he could win a real fossil (a crinoid stem). I had an appointment to get my hair cut that day and so we had this conversation:

"Jimmy, you are going to have to go back to After School Care now. I have to leave."

"Where are you going?"

"I am going to the beauty shop."

"What's that?"

"It is a place where ladies go to get their hair cut and to get beautiful."

After careful consideration, he looked at me and asked,

"Does that mean that when I see you tomorrow, you won't look like you do today?"

The Contest

My classroom was across the hall from the bath-
rooms. Sometimes I had to go in them to check
on things. One day there was a lot of noise coming out of the boys' bathroom. I stood outside
and listened for a while, and when things kept
getting noisier and noisier, I announced that I
was coming in. I walked in, and found a group of
boys standing back against the stalls facing the
urinals. I stood and looked at them and asked,

"Who won?"

They all pointed with pride at Mitchell who was
standing WAY FAR BACK with a grin on his face.
I stood there for a minute, and then sent them
all back to their rooms....except Mitchell. I sent
him to get a mop. That grin quickly disappeared,
and I guess that might have been the reason that

I got a beautifully decorated, but unsigned card on my birthday that year. The card was in Mitchell's handwriting and read . . .

"Happy birthday great, big, fat, hairy Mrs. Pattillo.

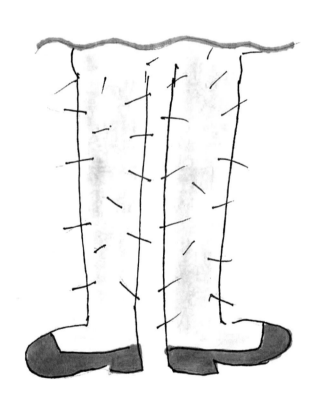

He was one of a kind ...

Once I found a note on my desk telling me that Ricky's dad would be coming to pick him up at noon to take him to the dentist. I invited Ricky to step into the hall with me for a word. I told him that I would be going down to the office with him when his dad came, and that I was going to tell his dad these things:

1. "You never do any of your work."

2. "You talk constantly."

3. "When I'm not looking you hop up and flip somebody on the head."

4. "You leave the room without permission, and I have to send someone to find you."

5. "The other day you asked to go to the bathroom, and we found you in the library."

14

6. "And, this very morning, the bus driver was up here complaining about your behavior on the bus."

He looked at me , took a deep breath and replied,

"My daddy is going to kill you!

The secret to teaching is in knowing how to communicate ...

"Mrs. Pattillo, there was this boy and he died when he was only 16."

"Did you know him?"

"No."

"When did this happen?"

"A long time ago."

"How did you know about it?"

"That's what it said."

Have you been visiting the cemetery?"

"No, we went to the graveyard."

"Mrs. Pattillo, that girl said 'So what' to my privacy."

"She said what?"

"So what to my privacy"

"What privacy"?

"You know, like when you want to be alone."

"Okay, start from the top, and tell me everything that was said."

" I said, 'I need some privacy,' and she said,

'So what?'"

* * *

"What do you mean you bit his butt 'on a accident'? Did his butt fly across the playground and hit you in the mouth?"

18

"You know that stuff that makes you sick"?

"A virus"?

"No, that green stuff."

"Green snot?"

"No, that stuff that gets on your car."

"Pollen?"

"Yep, we had it on our mirror this morning." AT

* * *

"Mrs. Pattillo, Mrs. Pattillo, come quick!"

"What's the matter?"

"Jacob was standing on the toilet, and he fell off, and hit his head, and broke it!"

"He broke his head?"

"No, he broke the toilet!"

"Billy, go tell the lunchroom lady to send me some butter so this poor child here doesn't have to spend the rest of his life on the playground with his thumb stuck in this hole."

* * *

"Mrs. Ross, would you like for Emily to help you carry these things to your car?"

Emily: "Mumble, mumble, mumble."

"What did you say?"

Emily: "I said, 'You sure are good at volunteering other people's services.'"

* * *

"I'm going to say this once. You are not going to walk around this room at reading time today. Go and sit in that white chair until I tell you that you can get up."

"Do you want me to read?"

"If this talking keeps up, I'm going to make this whole class walk laps at recess."

Voice from the back of the room...
"You can do that? Man! when I grow up I am going to be a teacher!" TF

"Okay, now when we go to recess today, you people who have been complaining that you are too sick to work, can sit on the 'I'm too sick to play' bench unless, of course, you experience a miraculous recovery."

"I did! I did! I had one of those coveries."

* * *

"Tell me again how you managed to get your head stuck in the hole in the back of your chair."

Some complicated instruction ...

"Mrs. Pattillo, what's an adjective?"
"Mrs. Pattillo, what's an adjective?"
"Mrs. Pattillo, what's an adjective?"

"Never mind him, Mrs. Pattillo, he is just trying to aggravate you."

"No, you don't understand, I really haven't been listening and paying attention..." GD

* * *

"If a word problem says 'and' then you add. If the problem says 'were left' or 'are left', then you subtract."

"What if it says, 'and a?'"

"Who knows what snakes do in the wintertime?"

"I know! I know! They hyperventilate" TG

* * *

"Now boys and girls, when you finish writing your story, I want you to read it out loud, and every time your voice stops, put a period."

Puzzled student: "Just how does that work?"

* * *

"If you have seven noses, and each nose has four boogers, how many boogers will you have?" AR

Field Trips

You can certainly learn a lot on a field trip..if you sit beside the right kid on the bus.

As Chattanooga came into view:

"I can tell that is New York because it has those big towers." AM

* * *

"Yesterday we went to the Chattanooga Natchur Sinner. Ryan found some skunk feathers." BB

* * *

"Mrs. Pattillo, is it okay if my mama goes only half way on the field trip?"

"Why would she only want to go half way?"

"She don't have much gas in her car."

Do you see that house over there?
Well, a boy lived there who got killed by a truck.

"Did you know him?"

"No, my mama heard it on the newspaper."

* * *

"Michelle, look over there. Do you see all of those tall buildings? That is Chattanooga."

"Which one?" ML

Questions, questions, questions ...

"Mrs. Pattillo, how do you spell 'poachers'?"

"Tell me your sentence."

"The poachers went to Bethlehem and killed all the babies. We saw a movie about it at church."

* * *

"Mrs. Pattillo, did Jesus grow up to be a missionary?"

* * *

"Mrs. Pattillo, what is the name of the new Wal*Mart?"

* * *

"Faith, you have a very beautiful name."

"Well, do you read your Bible? It's in there." FC

* * *

"Look at my picture. Do you see those mountains in the background? I colored them purple, like in the song. I think I'll color a fruited plain right there. What is a fruited plain, anyway?" GD

"Did Dr. Martin Luther King, Jr. go to heaven when he died?"

"I'm pretty sure that he did. He was a preacher after all."

"Do teachers go to heaven when they die?"

"I hope so. When I get there I am going to ask God for the job of passing out homework at the Pearly Gates."

"You mean there is homework in heaven? Ahh, you are just teasing. God wouldn't let you do that." A

The dog did what?

Sometimes it really is hard to keep a straight face, especially when excuses for not doing homework are involved.

"My Mama didn't have time to do my homework last night."

"Why didn't you do it?"

"I didn't have time either".

* * *

"Okay, let's hear it. Where is your homework today?"

"I left it on the china cabinet."

"Well, that is 43 times you have left that homework on the china cabinet. You need to come in here with a better story tomorrow."

The next day......

"Bring me your homework, please."

"I don't have it."

30

"Where is it today? Is it on the china cabinet again?"

"Nope, you told me not to tell you that anymore."

"Well, where is it?"

"It fell out of my pocket while I was repelling up a mountain." DG

In my opinion ...

"Kids need homework so they can learn about stuff like pronouns. Then when they get to ninth grade like my sister, they will know about them. My sister knows all about pronouns." SD

"Homework is good for kids. If they have homework they will not be dome." DW

"If kids did not have homework, they would not be smart, but they would be happy."

It's The Rule !

We have rules that we have to follow all through life. Some are for school and some...... are not.

"If your mama leaves the room, don't drink her beer."

It's the rule!

"Don't chase your mother's car down the street, she will just bring you back to school."

It's the rule!

"Empty the worms out of your pockets before you come in the building."

It's the rule!

"If you give your mother a quarter, your freckles will disappear for a week."

It's the rule!

"If teachers paddle kids, the kids can sue them for all their pennies."

Good luck with that one.

"You always have to follow the constructions."

It's the rule!

"Kids have the right to remain silent."

Hah!

"No farting during the blessing."

IT'S THE RULE!

35

When I grow up ...

Every year I would have the children write and decorate booklets called, "When I Grow Up". Not everybody wants to be a superhero.

The Artist...

"Mrs. Pattillo, I don't know how to decorate my book cover."

"Well, what do you want to be when you grow up?"

I want to be an artist."

Well, draw things that artists use, like brushes, paint, and easels."

"You don't understand, I can't draw."

The Paleontologist....

"When I grow up I am going to be a finder bones. You know, those people who dig in the dirt and find dinosaurs and stuff." PH

The Director...

"I am going to make movies when I grow up. This is how you do it. You have to be very mean.
You yell, 'Seam 1, ACCHUN!'
You yell, 'Seam 2, ACCHUN!'
At the end you yell, 'Cut!'" BB

Attention NFL!

"I am going to be a football player. Sometimes you get thron in the mud. You get a lot of broozes. You wiar a lot of pads. If you get thrown a rond, you get mad and jump up and nock somebody down." BS

The Lawyer...

"When I grow up I am going to be a looyer. They tell people what to do like, 'Come in here now.' And they do it, belive me. Looyers get to say things like , 'Go get me coffee, please'" SD

The Singer

"When I grow up I am going to be a singer, and sing rocken roll songs like 'Putt a Little Dime in the Juke Box, Baby'" SD

The Builder

"When I grow up I am going to be a builder. If you don't follow the constructions then you will be fired." KS

The Policewoman

"When I grow up I am going to be a policewoman because there is a lot of axshone. I love axshone." SD

The Marine

"I am going to be a Marine. Marines get in a lot of mud. They are real strong. They can swim good, and they sleep in fox holes." NS

The Cosmetologist

"When I grow up I am going to be a make up speulalist, and poot make up on movie stars. But first I have to practice on my Aunt Sharlene." SC

The Teacher

"When I grow up I am going to be a teacher. Then I can boss kids around, and eat candy behind their backs."

(Don't look at me!)

Holidays

The elementary school calendar revolves around holidays . You only need to look at the art work and stories displayed on the walls to know what time of year it is.

Columbus Day

"Christopher Columbus sailed across the ocean. There were bad stuff in that ocean. The people said, 'Have you lost your mind?'" CE

Thanksgiving

"A long time ago everybody went across the Atlantic Ocean. They went to the new world where there were Indians behind the trees. The King rode in the Mayflower, and the Pilgrims rode in the Speedwell. All the Pilgrims ate corn, and baked deer and turkey and fish. In the fall they invited the Indians over. That was the first Thanksgiving."

"The pilgrims got tired of werking for the king, so they hopped on the Mayflower and left."

* * *

"Squanto showed the Pilgrims how to make corn with fish."

Christmas

"Once there was a kid named Jesus and a king named Herod. Jesus had a mom and a dad named Joseph and Mary. One year Mary and Joseph went to Bethlehem and there was no room so they had to stay in a manger. There were some animals , too. There was one donkey, a cow, some horses, sheep, and a dove. An angel told Joseph to "leave the manger", so Mary and Joseph headed to Egypt. They stayed in Egypt until Herod died. Then Jesus grew up to be the savior of the world. That is the real story of Christmas." Tucker

The Story of Christmas

"There was a time when Merry and Joseph got married. Then an angel came and told Merry that she would have a baby. His name would be Jesus. Merry went to see Joseph, but he was not at home, so she waited for him and when he got home then she tolled him the good news. They decided to go to Bethlaham. Joseph lifted Merry up on a camel. They tried to find a stable but they could not." Kayla

Dr. King's Birthday

"Dr. Martin Luther King, Jr. was a great man. He became a leader and a normal preacher Then he told the speech. He had a dream about everyone being equal."

Presidents' Day

"Abraham Lincoln fitted for the Silver War. He had a famous speech. He got killed while he was watching a movie in the Ford Theater."

Valentine's Day

You can get a valentine to be yours if you take this advice:

"Try saying, "Would you merry me?""

"Mail them a secret admier letter."

"Tell them love stories."

"Always look cute."

"Buy them jewelry."

"Put a love note in their desk."

"Pay attinchen to them."

"Choklets usually work."

"Give them a ring with three dimends."

"Take them to a fansy resterrent in a limo."

"Chase them on the playground."

Easter

"I'll tell you the story of Easter. One day Jesus was jest doing nothing, and God said, 'Jesus, will you die for all my people so they can come to Heaven when they die? You can rise in three days, and we will call it Easter.' And so it was done. They put a thorn crown on him. They locked him on a cross and cakrafieed him. And then a day later a soldier came and stuck him with a spear, and hit him in the side of the rib. Poor, poor, poor, poor, poor Jesus. And then the Easter Bunny knew what to do. So he sprang into action. He painted eggs and put them in a basket. Then he came on Easter to each house every year." Kayla F.

"We had a big egg hunt on Easter. I font eleven hard eggs, and two plastic ones. A lady said that if you sit on an egg you will grow a chickin. When I sat on it I broke it. Then I stold everyone's chocolate eggs. I had the bestest Easter!"

The Tattle Box

One year I put a tattle box in the back of the room. It was for non emergency tattles (those not involving tears, blood, or safety). After school I would read all the little scraps of paper to see what had really been going on in the classroom that day. I don't know how I missed it all.

Tattle 1

"Jimmy was being a smatelic."

Tattle 2

"Abby called me a recard."

Tattle 3

"Lucy is looking at other peoples' privesy in the bathroom."

Tattle 4

"Danny sed he would poot my I ball up my butt hol."

Tattle 5
"Taylor said I am dummer than him."

Tattle 6
"Nate called me a poopee head."

Tattle 7
"Amy hit me on my shots."

Tattle 8
"Jeffry sed the E word (ediot)."

Tattle 9
"Zach horse played in the bathroom."

Tattle 10
"Joe was standing on the toolit in the bathroom."

Tattle 11
"Allie always wants her way."

Tattle 12
"Sam said crap, and pain in the you know what and something elts!"

Tattle 13
"Shane goes, 'Blob, blob, blob', when I try to talk."

Tattle 14
"Jenny has some candy, and she gave one to Kallie, and she don't have enuff for everyone. 5-06-04 Love, Mandy."

Tattle 15
"Serina has gum in her maoth."

Tattle 16
"Some one riht on my desc."

Tattle 17
"Imle cold me stuped."

Tattle 18

"Libby said some cus wurkes."

Tattle 19

"Matthew is tadaling on me about things that are his falt!"

Tattle 20

"Jason sed that I was flirting with him. He made me mad!"

Tattle 21

"Ellie is not being a good spoat."

Tattle 22

"Tyler said my teeth were brown."

Tattle 23

"David kofed in my face."

Tattle 24

"Bobby is bothering me. Thanks."

Tattle 25

"I didn't do it! I didn't! I didn't! I didn't, but Tammy did. She pushed me, and smacked me in the face! I'm telling the turth!"

Tattle 26

"Nikki called me a doo doo head."

Tattle 27

"Jacob puchst 15 cids."

Tattle 28

"Bryan said ass hol."

Tattle 29

"Everybody"

And that is about the size of it.

Through the eyes of a child ...
(and right out of his mouth)

Children see their teachers in many different ways, and they don't mind telling you what they think about what they see. One year Hallmark* offered mugs for Valentine's Day with the head of a certain grouchy old lady on them. I got three. During the party one of my kids wandered up to my desk and with a puzzled look on his face asked,

"Where did people get those cups with you on them?"

* * *

Mama, my teacher is funny. Say something funny, Mrs. Pattillo."

* * *

"I liked your hair better the other color."

* * *

"Are you going to have a baby or are you just fat?"

"Did you know you have hairs in your nose?"

* * *

"You may look old, but you are not. Happy birthday."

* * *

"Happy birthday. I can't draw that much candles."

* * *

"So, you are 54. I am surprised that you are still alive."

* * *

"You are grouchy today. I think you need some chocolate."

* * *

"You have wrinklees there, and wrinklees there, and wrinklees there."

* * *

When you were little did you have a pet dinosaur?"

"My teacher has a hard time solving crimes."

* * *

"My teacher is mean. When you are late she says, 'I thought you were dead'. She gives you a poisonas kiss on your birthday. When you talk she will put a stick in your pocket. She gives me a lot of sticks."

"You are too old for this job."

* * *

And then there was the child who was writing a story about her year in second grade. She came up to my desk and asked me to spell <u>wonderful</u>, <u>teacher</u>, and <u>universe</u>. As she walked away, I added, "Don't forget skinny and gorgeous." The finished story read:

"My teacher is the best and most wonderful teacher in the universe and Tunnel Hill. She thinks she is skinny and gorgeous, but she is not." KR

55

Is your daddy named God?

There was a boy in my class named Jesus. One day another child looked at his name tag and realized, for the first time, how his friend's name was spelled. He then asked in all seriousness, "Is your daddy named God?" Jesus just looked puzzled and went back to his desk. When I got control of myself (under the desk again), I tried to explain about the spelling, but it was too late. The news had spread. A few days later the secretary called on the intercom and asked that Jesus be sent to the office because his daddy was there to get him. Every head in that room went up. I asked if she would send Jesus's daddy down to the classroom for a minute. When he got there I explained that there was a rumor going around that Jesus's daddy was named God, and the children wanted to see what he looked like. He stood there a minute (maybe considering his promotion), and then roared with laughter. I'll bet that man is still laughing.

Second grade theology

"If Paul Revere was a silversmith, and the person who makes horseshoes is a blacksmith, then God must be a peoplesmith!"

* * *

"God has a hard job. He spends a lot of time trying to control the devil. Mostly he werks at night and sleeps during the day."

* * *

"Everyday God has to tell the angels what to do. When he gets finished with that, he answers a few prayers."

* * *

"God's job is to make new people and to watch the ones he has already made. He sits on a rock (of ages?) and wears a crown."

* * *

Once upon a time teachers were allowed to pray in our schools. Everyday, as we lined up for lunch I would thank God for our food, and

I would add "and God, take care of all the children who are sick and couldn't be at school today." I guess that Jessica got tired of the same old prayer everyday so one day she asked if she could pray. This is her prayer:

"Thank you, God, that it didn't rain at recess today.
Thank you for all the great things in the world.
Thank you for not killing us yet."

**Now I ask you ...
Is your daddy named God?**

Oh give me a home, some relatives, and some killer cats.

School is home for most of the day, but when that big yellow bus pulls out in the afternoon, it takes kids into another dimension (sort of like that show on TV, you know which one). Snippets! Snippets! That is all the information you ever get from that place. Sometimes even snippets are too much.

"My grandmother is fancy. If I get a drop of apple juse on her floor she will mop it up quick!"

* * *

"My family went to Galenbird (Gatlinburg). We stayed in a caben and my bathroom had a jadoocee." SD

* * *

"My house is full of kids. Mean ones, too. They are Jason and Caroline and Susie and Billy. I live there, too."

* * *

"My house is gray. It is brown, too. It is a little trashy, but at least it keeps me out of the rain."

"My dad's name is Randy, but that is just his step name. His real name is Randal." RH

* * *

"My grandmother is mean. She don't have musuls at all. They flop down every time. Bulev me. I've seen it happen. She is very gripy, but I love her." AP

* * *

"I can tell when my mother is mad. She gets her mad face. Her eyes get real big, and she turns red. Then the yelling starts."

* * *

"I'm getting checked out early today."

"Why?"

"I'm going to the doctor."

"What's wrong with you?"

"My brother thinks my nerves are shot." BB

"Did you put this note on Nate's desk?"
"Uh huh."
"Did you write the word 'asshole'?"
"Yep"
"How did you know how to spell it?"
"My mama teached me."

* * *

"Why are you so sleepy today?"
"Because my mama got me up at the butt crack of dawn."

* * *

"My mamaw is teaching me those rhymes that you learn at church. I think they are called Bible verses. I would tell you one, but I forgot." GD

* * *

"Last night I went to church to see my friend get bathbutised. When she got out of that bath thing she was cold." HF

* * *

"On my winter break I got into a fite with my sister. I got in trouble because of her like I do all the time. I wish my mom would sell her sometimes."

"My mama is coming to eat lunch with me today. I hope it gets dark before lunch because I wore my new 'glow in the dark' tee shirt."

* * *

Title of a picture done at art time:
"My cousin Rudy in gel."

* * *

"My mama is going to Chatsworth this weekend. Every time she goes down there she gets pregnant."

* * *

"Mrs. Pattillo, I don't know who my grandmother is."

"Yes, you do. Her name is Lorraine."

"No, Lorraine is my grandma. You told me to write about my grandmother." KD

* * *

"We went to Florida. We went on the inerstak. We went to my daddy's girlfriend's cusing's house and then to her granmol's house." HC

"I have some cats at my house. I saw my cats sitting beside a cild rabbit. I know they did it, because there were scratch marks on the rabbit the same size as my cats' claws." ED

* * *

"Our class made a play out of a story, and my grandmother came to see it. She said it was the best. She said we were born actors. We had seven parts and four main characters, so we had to have three casts to get everybody in. I was the narrator in cast three. My grandmother said if we did another play she would not miss it, but only if I was in cast one. I do not know why she said that, but it was funny to me. I laughed and laughed. She did not laugh." Jennifer Q.

Snippets, Snippets, & More Snippets!

"My head is just full of poems!" BB

* * *

"Guess what! I just got myself an idea!" GD

* * *

"That computer is a lying dog! It said I made a 60 on that A.R. test, and I know I made 100!" BC

* * *

"I always make 100 on my A.R. tests because I read my book so many times I rememorize it."

* * *

"My mama said that my great- grandpa had a heart tag."

* * *

"Did you know that a snake will slither up your leg if you poke it long enough?"

* * *

"The capital of Georgia is 'G'."

"Look! When you put the words in alphabetical order, they go the way the ABC's go!" GD

* * *

Four ways to write 14

"7+7, 14, ___, ___ " DD

A+

* * *

"Dinosaurs had a hard life. They got berried in tar or kwiksand. Then they got hit by a meteor."

* * *

"Cavemen were dumb. They tried to drive a car with square wheels." JT

* * *

"A fossil is a bone that is deid." SD

* * *

"Bellybuttons hold your legs on." MM

"A salary is a number of money." EC

* * *

"Grown-ups should not have mouths. Then they couldn't tell you to take out the garbage." RH

* * *

"A toadstool is a stool that has bumps on it." TS

* * *

"Kids should not have to ride the bus because it makes you go to sleep and miss your school,
and when you wake up you are at the high school." SD

* * *

"Thunder happens when God hits the clouds together." BN

* * *

"The tooth fairy sneaks into your room and steals your tooth. Then she gives it to her husband to make dentures for old people." NM

"Teacher, when center time comes, I want to play with those George Washington logs." HB

***

"Good grief! If I had known I was going to have to do this much work, I would have stayed at home." ML

***

"Dear Techer, Beth can not come to school and the re-sun is cause she is sidk. Love, Beth"

***

On field day: "We will do the kangaroo hop when they bring us the kangas." PH

A few days after a character lesson on the meaning of the word integrity, I saw a child crawling on the floor around the room. I started fussing:

"Ryan!" I yelled, "Get up off that floor right now, and get back in your seat. What on earth has come over you?"

Never one to let an injustice slide, Ryan marched up to my desk, looked me in the eye, and declared:

"BUT YOU DON'T UNDERSTAND! I was picking up paper when nobody was looking. I was doing that integrity stuff!" RL

* * *

One day at recess a little boy came up to visit with me. He told me his life story, and then said that he couldn't talk to me anymore because he had to go take care of some business on the playground. When I asked what that was, he answered:

"I've got to go out there and beat the crap out of a few people."

Sometimes I'd like to hire that kid.

A few last minute gifts for the world at Christmas

"I would give the world clothes, so people don't have to go around naked." CE

* * *

"I would give the world brothers and sisters , because nobody likes to play alone." KF

* * *

Matt: "If I could give the world a gift, I would give all people everlasting life."

Rose: "You can't do that because God already tried it."

Matt: "Uh huh, and it worked, too, didn't it?"

* * *

"My gift to the world would be to make people walk who are paralyzed. Then my daddy could walk again." BD

"I would give the world more schools so kids could lurn how to find words up in the dictionary." AB

* * *

"I would give the world peace, so other kids' sisters wouldn't bother them like mine does. I love peace." SD

Roll over James Pierpont

jing oil bells, jing oil bells,
jing oil all the way
o- woeat fun in easter
ride in a one hosoe open
slad Hay!

And now, boys and girls ...

We have come to the end of this little book; and since a teacher never stops being one, I would like to review what I hope we all have learned:

1. It will rain at recess sometimes. Don't let that keep you from playing.

2. Follow life's rules and constructions. That way you don't have so many regrets when you get to the jumping off place.

3. Give those around you your very best gifts, and ask God to take care of the hard stuff.

4. There are many ways to look at things. Consider them all before you take care of business on the playground of life.

5. Go the distance. Just hanging in there is often what gets the job done.

6. Sometimes you need to wade in where a sane person wouldn't go. Sanity is highly overrated.

7. Be willing to laugh at yourself, and you will never be too old for any job.

8. There are still great things in the world. Look around you.

9. Practice that integrity stuff.

10. Be kind, loving , and respectful to all people . You never know when you might run into Jesus's daddy.

Class dismissed

Thanks to:

Marilyn Byrd

Deborah Duncan

Kathryn Hendrix

Ann Johnston

Joan Jolley

Meredith Miller

Anne Monk

John Pattillo

Nancy Ross

Jean Whitfield

And to the sweet people who will always
remain just as I knew them at
Tunnel Hill Elementary

70216727R00046

Made in the USA
San Bernardino, CA
27 February 2018